COMPASSION

THOUGHTS ON CULTIVATING A GOOD HEART

COMPASSION

Compiled and introduced by
Amy Lyles Wilson

FRESH AIR BOOKS™
Nashville

Contents

INTRODUCTION
Amy Lyles Wilson

One Sunday I found myself sitting near Ben, a homeless man who visits our church on occasion. Although he is, for the most part, uncommunicative, I think he senses that our chapel is a place he can receive Communion and community. Most Sundays, though, Ben seems to do nothing more than sleep, slumped over a bit with his chin lowered to his chest.

On this particular morning, Ben appeared to be resting as usual. *What can he be getting out of this?* I wondered. *Maybe all he needs is an hour off the streets. Maybe he comes for the coffee and bagels.*

While I was nosing into someone else's business instead of minding my own, the pianist began playing a familiar hymn. Like many of my old favorites, the song quite often brings me to tears. And on this particular Sunday, when I was missing my dead father even more than usual, a few simple chords had the potential to make me weep. As I was reaching for a tissue in my purse, I heard a noise coming from Ben. He lifted his head only slightly, and his eyes remained closed. But his voice was sure and clear and strong. "Let us break bread together on our knees."

And there it was. After I stopped crying, I realized that I would never understand what brings Ben to church, and that it is not for me to reason why. Quite possibly he's driven by motivations I could never fathom, needs known only to God. As I was leaving the church, it hit me: I am not called to understand. Instead, I am called simply to make room on the pew and in my heart.

Compassion: Thoughts on Cultivating a Good Heart invites us to consider that our attention to the little things makes it easier to appreciate the concerns of our friends, families, communities, and the world at large. In so doing we can begin to conduct our lives with an ever-present spirit of compassion instead of saving such outpouring for tragic situations and natural disasters. The writers in this collection encourage us to suffer with those who are hurting so that we might relieve their pain and in the process heal ourselves as well. When we are in touch with the pain in the world, we increase our opportunities to serve others. I hope I remember that the next time I see Ben.

WHAT IS COMPASSION?
Melissa Tidwell

When my daughter was in junior high school, she had a social studies unit on world religions and for weeks we discussed the various beliefs of Hindus, Buddhists, and Christians. Suddenly I found myself defending the Christian position on the doctrines that I myself had sometimes questioned, an odd role for the rebellious skeptic I had always thought myself to be. My parents had been raised to be Baptists, or something stricter, but they let me find my own way, and I fled all the shouting and the altar calls for a more intellectual approach.

But now, as the daily ride to school with my daughter became the daily religious debate, I began to feel the prickly defensive fear that I had not done an adequate job of presenting the beauty of the Christian story and so was losing my child to the Buddhists.

Projection being my default setting for unwelcome information, I began to resent the subtle and insidious way Buddhism seemed to be creeping into the god-talk of many of my friends and loved ones. I remembered how my entire seminary community had lost its head when the Dalai Lama came for a conference being held at our campus and almost rioted when we were told we could not meet him. Now my daughter had joined the crowd, bringing home books by former members of other faiths who had found more peace as Buddhists. Well, I harrumphed, it's easy to be popular when all you talk about is something easy like *compassion*.

But as I grudgingly read the books scattered about the kitchen, which I now saw as a window into my daughter's heart, I noticed the way my own heart began to respond to this subtle shift in emphasis. Buddhism's noble truths identify human suffering as a reality, and for some readers the hard truth of suffering sends them skittering away looking for a happier truth. But those who continue past the first gate will find that the Buddhist response to suffering is compassion. It's not a promise of pie in the sky but a stance of profound respect and disciplined engagement.

The concept of compassion is not alien to Christianity, but it seems more popular with Buddhists. We Christians, instead, tend to speak of love. And love is powerful, to be sure. But love is murkier.

Love is confused, compromised, almost obscured by its many forms and contexts. Humans have a hard time keeping their love pure—we confuse eros, sensual love, with agape, selfless love; and we paste over a lot of hostility and passive-aggressive behavior by claiming to do things out of love.

Compassion on the other hand, seems a bit more pure for not having been dragged through the mud of many bad pop songs. Compassion is an earthling-to-earthling feeling, where love is the universal application, what you feel for God, country, friend, spouse, child, puppy, and the Boston Red Sox; all the same word.

Compassion has the added benefit of some kind of built-in cliché protector. Christians, or at least the modern Western variety, have badly misused the admonition to love the sinner but hate the sin. We cannot so easily put together a snappy phrase about compassion and sin, because there is no corresponding binary pair. Have compassion for the sinner but be indifferent to the sin? Can't quite imagine it on a T-shirt.

You may argue that Buddhism does not truly recognize the existence of sin and that the division between the two faiths should diverge right here, but I am not so sure. Contemporary Buddhist teacher Pema Chödrön talks about the hooks that snag and hold us from the attainment of real freedom. The pain of those hooks relates, at least for me, to the roots of the Hebrew word for sin, which I have heard explained as arrows that miss the mark. The source of those hooks and arrows is a force way so complex and sneaky powerful that the language of love and hate is no longer adequate. God told Cain that sin lurks outside the door, and the proper relationship of the faithful toward that lurking menace is probably something more in the range of a sober reckoning and cautious distance, the way one ought to deal with wild bears and those deep-fry turkey machines. There's no point in hating a bear for being wild, when in fact wildness is part of what makes us long to glimpse one out in the woods.

For all of Christianity's tough talk, many of us are secretly dazzled by sin, like one of the poor saps in those romantic comedies where an oblivious twosome fail to detect their obvious attraction and pretend to loathe the other while secretly falling deeply in—there we go again—love. Love and sin may be that couple, and their melodrama will play endlessly unless we can bear the pain of unhooking ourselves and finding a new way. That process of disengagement is painful, as most of us who have lived a long time on a merry-go-round of good intentions and failure can attest. To face the places where we have been scarred and to continue tracing our pain back to its source is precise, exacting, costly work, not for starry-eyed ingénues or clumsy bronco busters. Those places in the human heart where we hurt are precisely the places where we need compassionate care.

My experience has been that sinners respond a lot better to compassion than to self-righteousness. Because compassion is not understood as an emotion in the way love is, then feeling compassion is rightly seen (as love ought to be) as a choice, an attitude that is taken up with purpose and intention and held despite lapses, roadblocks, and difficulties. Compassion chosen in this way then becomes another form of spiritual practice, like meditation that is incredibly simple and endlessly difficult.

Spiritual practice is another one of the things I picked up on in reading Buddhist writers. Buddhists don't talk so much about being a certain kind of Buddhist but of having a certain kind of practice. A Buddhist would say, "I practice the tonglen meditation form," rather than "I am a tonglenian." It's a subtle difference but one that stresses an important truth: we don't just arrive at our faith and then never have to lift a finger again. It is always a work in progress.

The notion of practice asks us to define ourselves in terms that ancient Christians called a rule of life. How do I intend to live in response to my experience of God? What kind of person am I going to offer back to God in gratitude for my life? Not a Presbyterian life or a Lutheran life or a Baptist life but a baptized life. What a powerful witness that would be!

We should not choose our practice on the basis of style, though, or from convenience or even from aptitude. Our practice comes to us as a calling, perhaps even a gift, though with a great deal of assembly required. If we choose to talk about compassion because we like the way it sounds, then we are making an empty sound at best. Words have power. Naming correctly what we want our spiritual practice to become gives us the chance to be more conscious about how our intentions shape our actions. And striving for compassion reminds us to look for the opportunities to practice compassion. In this way we take up the challenge to be the change in the world we want to see.

Being the change reminds me of an old friend with whom I liked to swap stories of the unintentionally wonderful things our children said, like my daughter's lament that I had "misunderheard" her. My friend's young daughter in the same way had admonished her mother after the mother had been forced to mete out some discipline. "Mom, you were not compassion with me." This little linguistic slip stuck with me because it left me with the sobering thought that I might in fact be all the compassion a person ever knows. It is simply not enough to have an abstract compassion in our hearts that has no embodiment in the messy world of heartbreak and misunderhearing. We must act out our compassion. We must *be* compassion.

Jesus was compassion. He was moved by the crowds who followed him across the lake, and he asked his disciples to share their food with the people. He was moved by the faith of those who sought him for healing; and he touched them, got close, kneeled in the dust, wept. He did not practice his compassion from afar but expressed it at the dinner table with learned intellectuals, in the boat with fishermen, on the road as he walked, even, the Gospels tell us, as he hung on the cross.

How do we embody compassion? One way is to decide that everybody counts. I recall being shocked during a conversation about a global issue when the person I was speaking with said, "I just don't have the time to care about those people over there. We have suffering people over here in our country too." I suspect this was a defense mechanism, that the person feared that opening her heart to those who live in other places would overwhelm her capacity to continue. I understand such fear, but I think that the antidote to such fear is not less compassion, but more. Being more respectful of other human beings and their pain means we cannot simply choose where to spend our compassion, as if we were dining in a cafeteria. The interconnection of the human family, even the complex connections of the global economy, require us to take notice of the others sharing the planet and its resources. Small actions, like learning to properly pronounce another's name, show the respect that underlies compassion. Yes, it can be complicated, and there is too much suffering in the world for us to work toward righting every wrong. But knowing where Darfur is on the map can signal a prayerful concern and remind the head and heart to work together, so that our compassion produces both inward and outward expressions of our concern.

Compassion is the recognition that we all matter, which means we have to make the courageous decision that we will care and act and not allow our wellspring of compassion to be drawn down too low or to be engulfed by despair. It means having the strength not to numb out when the suffering around us seems overwhelming but to courageously face both the pain and the beauty of living.

Above all, compassion means giving up on the idea of faith as yet another self-improvement process, one that will make us richer or thinner or more stylish or whatever we think we need to be complete. To have a compassionate heart for the world includes accepting the simple but difficult truth that the cycle of sin and hate is a kind of narcissism, a tomb from which Jesus wants to resurrect us. On the other side of it, our weaknesses and wounds are the holy places where the tender power of God can come close and transform us if we wish.

SEEING WITH OUR SOULS
Marilyn Brown Oden

The art of compassion is all about seeing with our souls. When we see with our souls, we become more aware of God's daily presence. We discover that we do not have to seek the cosmic dance. It comes to us through the simple gifts God offers us: the morning silence before words and works begin. The songs of birds greeting the dawn. The child who tugs on our sleeve and invites us, "Come see." The full orange moon shining through the trees. We look through the eyes of Psalm 103: "God touches all in the heavens and on earth. Everything is full of sacred presence." We begin to realize that anything that happens to us—*anything*—can become a means to spiritual growth. We glimpse what Joan Chittister is talking about when she says, "Everything I do today carries within it a flash of the divine."[1]

~

I attended a Bible study led by Evelyn Laycock [where] she told an ancient story:

A seeker asked a Wise One: "When will the dawn come? Will it come when I can tell a sheep from a dog?"

"No," said the Wise One. "It will not come when you can tell a sheep from a dog."

"Will it come when I can tell the difference between two kinds of trees?"

"No," said the Wise One. "It will not come when you can tell the difference between two kinds of trees."

"Then when will the dawn come?"

The Wise One answered, "The dawn will come when you can see each person as your sister or your brother."

To see with our souls is to greet the dawn. It is to meet our brothers and sisters where they are and to treat them as though they are already what they can be. The old habitual question "How do I feel when I'm with you?" is exchanged for a new one: "How do you feel when you're with me?" We listen and respond to the other as we would to the Christ.

But how many others? Our brothers and sisters extend around the world. Who is to be in our immediate circle of care? Like the Benedictines, anyone who comes to our door? Everyone we see? What about people in the workplace and grocery store? On the tollway? Caring for others is not something on a to-do list, prescribing a certain number of people and associated with duty. It relates to a natural response to God's love. If we listen to our hearts, we will know who is in our basket of responsibility in a given moment.

Seeing with our souls nourishes a spiritual attitude. Or perhaps it is the other way around, and a spiritual attitude nourishes our capacity to see with our souls. The phrase *spiritual attitude* can easily be misunderstood. It does not mean pomposity and showy piety. It does not mean ignoring the complexity of today's world. It does not mean limiting faith to a rigid set of "right" rules. We are on the wrong spiritual attitude track if we would rather be right than helpful.

Back in the fifth century, some "right rule" kind of folk came to see Abba Poemen, one of the desert fathers. "Tell us," they said, "when we see brothers dozing during the sacred office, should we pinch them so they will stay awake?"

The old man responded: "Actually, if I saw a brother sleeping, I would put his head on my knees and let him rest."

That is seeing with our souls. It is compassion. It is being a healing presence, a channel of blessing.

How much people need a healing presence! In his book *The Wounded Heart of God*, Andrew Sung Park speaks of *han*.[2] It is a Korean word that, roughly translated, means "the pain of being victimized." *Han* can be described as a physical wound, "the division of the tissue of the heart caused by abuse, exploitation, and violence. It is the wound to feelings and self-dignity." *Han* is a kind of pain that brings forth shame.

This kind of pain is universal—all of us have experienced it to a greater or lesser degree. But in severe situations, it can permeate the very core of a person's existence. Park says, "In the life of han-ridden people, the mode of han overwhelms the other types of human emotion and becomes a domineering spirit." He suggests that the healing of *han* calls for "the negation of the negation."

Recently I visited an elementary school. As I entered a classroom, I noticed that construction-paper sunflowers decorated the walls and a student's baby picture was in the center of each flower. A boy named Faruch, a refugee from the Balkans, was at the science table watching some caterpillars. Another boy wanted his place and jeered, "Faruch, you can't always have your way!"

I've been in Gornji Vakuf, Faruch's hometown. Two-story homes line the streets—some scarred with bullet holes, others caved in from bombs. I've seen camouflaged tanks and soldiers, heard the shelling and the bombers overhead, as Faruch must have time and time again. I've listened to the stories of women in the Balkan refugee centers. Women whose possessions had been reduced to the little bundle they'd been able to carry. Women who lived with awareness that their missing husbands or sons or fathers were probably among those murdered, their bodies thrown into mass graves.

Remember the sunflowers with baby pictures decorating the classroom wall? The center of Faruch's flower is empty. His mom couldn't flee with the family albums.

Faruch, you can't always get your way! I think he knows that. Faruch shows us *han*, for he has known victimization, violence, and negation.

❧

Listening is vital to journeying in compassion with one who is suffering. Brother David Steindl-Rast provides insight for us all when he writes about the monastic vow of obedience:

> The real task is learning to listen. The very word *obedience* comes from *ob-audire*, which means to listen intently. Its opposite is to be utterly deaf, and the word for this is literally *ab-surdus*. Everything is absurd until we learn to listen to its meaning; until we become "all ears" in obedience.
>
> In order to listen, you have to be silent.[3]

How contrary this is to our tendency to give advice to the sufferer! We mean well. We want to help. But unasked-for advice implies superiority and demonstrates our own impatience. We draw conclusions before listening to the story.

Recently I was with a group that had been invited to attend a clergy gathering at Camp Poust, a retreat center in the Czech Republic. My friend Marcus was lecturing on the importance of listening in pastoral care. As he spoke, the sound of a keyboard, played by an eight-year-old boy, drifted out through the open window of his room. A baby cried. A duck quacked. The leaves danced with the sun as it traveled from one side of the double-trunked tree to the other as Marcus taught. His native language is German, and he was trying to make himself understood both by those who spoke Czech and those who spoke English. When he talked about the insensitivity of poor listening, he used the phrase *not right in our ears*.

We want to be "right in our ears" when we journey with another person in compassion. Compassion calls us to set aside our stereotypes and be totally attentive to understanding another's language, that silent and anguished language of pain that longs for a response that will negate negation. It is as though we climb up a steep mountain, tethered together—not to carry the other but to be a strong, gentle presence that can help break a fall.

Have you ever walked around a large sculpture or tree to look at it from different perspectives? That is part of what we do when we see with our souls: We broaden our perspective. For if our passion for one point of view deafens us to others, how can we hear the whisper of Mystery that teaches us compassion?

When we see with our souls, we look beyond a single, limited perspective, especially in world situations, for those who have the power to tell the story generally shape popular perceptions. And there is always something more beyond.

We are not always capable of seeing with our souls—of being an instrument of compassion, a healing presence, a channel of blessing. But at times we are, and those are precious times. In those moments we become a living icon of God, a window through which others can glimpse God's love. Often small children show us how. Our granddaughter Chelsea was three years old when my husband's father died. At the service she sat between Bill and me. Sensing his sorrow—listening to the language of his heart—she snuggled close to him, put her tiny hand on his, looked up at him, and whispered, "I love you, Granddad." She offered healing presence. In that moment she was a window to God's love.

Each day offers us an opportunity to journey in compassion with our sisters and brothers and, through God's grace, to be windows through which others can see God's love. When we experience God's transforming love and our lives reflect it, we see with our souls.

To weep
with those who suffer
does not mean
that we have a good cry
and get on with other things.
It is more that we have a good cry
and we are never the same.

—JAN JOHNSON, A GOOD CRY

CAPACITY FOR COMPASSION
James C. Fenhagen

An increased capacity for compassion—the ability "to suffer with another's pain . . . comes about as the result of an increased sense of solidarity with the human family of which we are a part. When [the apostle] Paul talks about "suffering with those who suffer," he is talking about compassion, that supreme gift without which we are less than fully human. It might well be that the greatest threat to human survival now confronting us is not the loss of energy or the increase of pollution, but the loss of compassion. We are confronted daily with the pain of human tragedy—the breakup of a family or the sunken face of a starving child—to such an extent that we soon learn to turn off what we see. In order to cope with our feelings of helplessness, we teach ourselves how *not* to feel. The tragedy in this response, which is probably more widespread than we dare believe, is that we also deaden our capacity for love. For Christians, the cross stands as an ever-present reminder that love and suffering are two sides of the same coin.

OFFERING SILENT PRESENCE
Charles A. Parker

On a lonely Saturday night in July 1996, a young woman full of life and energy, a "successful pastor," lost her fight with depression. Locking up her parsonage, she drove to a nearby town, checked into a motel, and killed herself. I had known her since we had been in seminary together, where she had been a good student with a deep love of outdoor ministry. She spoke easily of God's call and seemed to take great joy in the people around her.

About two years before her death, I shared with her my own struggle with depression, and she likewise opened up to tell me of hers. During much of the year that followed that mutual revelation, we stayed in fairly regular contact, sharing stories of counseling and medication and the struggle of trying to find God amidst the never-distant pain. "Why did God create us this way?" "Could we rid ourselves of the suffering with more faith, more prayer?" Gradually, we spoke less often, as distance and newer commitments crowded out the older ones. She always felt guilty about "needing medication," so I assume that she must have stopped taking it. But she didn't call that night. There was no final desperate call, no plea for help. Just silence.

Sharing the pain of another person is a deeply humbling task, in large part because there are simply no words that can make the pain go away. When the people we love pour out the woundedness of their hearts before us, our love and empathy—and our egos—yearn to respond with words of comfort, words that can make sense of it all. But, as those who have known deep pain can witness, words cannot approach the place of suffering. They cannot stem the flow of anguish and grief. They are powerless. They are as ineffectual as using stones to dam a spring: the water will find some way to the surface.

The message of the cross is that God, through Christ, is present with us in our suffering. Simply saying that—even knowing it—does not take the pain away. Pain is still pain.

Yet, for the community of faith, . . . that message has profound significance. It means that we must be where Christ is—present with the suffering person. Simply present. Not trying to explain the

suffering, not to offer the platitudes of our clichéd wisdom, just to be.
In silence.

This too is a humbling task. Silence is a frightening and
vulnerable place to be, and it seems far too little to offer the one in
pain. But when we can put aside our ego's need to control the
situation, the need to be the savior ourselves, we open the space for the
Savior to come in a power that far exceeds all we can ask or imagine.
In silence, the One who suffers with us and who redeems our suffering
becomes present.

COMPASSION FOR ONESELF
Robert Corin Morris

"**N**ew occasions teach new duties," says an old hymn, and new occasions sometimes evoke from us aspects of the self we didn't imagine were there.[1] If we do not show hospitality to those elements of ourselves that are within, we may miss a call of God.

For one woman, aching wrists signaled a need to befriend an aspect of herself. Nearing midlife, Karen felt stalled in her spiritual growth. On the verge of serious depression, she was plagued by incipient arthritis. As we explored some of the ways she had experienced a sense of sacredness in her early life, she remembered the love she once had for drawing.

Why had she given it up? In her family, drawing wasn't considered serious enough to waste time on, so she'd pursued it on the margins of her life. She'd tried to do some drawing in college but had fallen in with a crowd of serious companions who ridiculed her efforts. So she'd turned her attention to the matters she had been schooled to regard as truly important, eventually going into the ministry . . . in a denomination that prized clear thinking and worthy social action.

As we talked, her wrists ached. Of course, it might be arthritis, but could this be the ache of heart and hands that wanted to draw? It took Karen a while to summon the courage to pick up a pencil, so deeply had she internalized the unloving rejection of her artistic self. When she finally did start to draw again, a cascade of images emerged. She moved into pastels. Her hands dug into fresh clay and shaped images of her own soul and then of the Holy. She loved what she was doing, and she loved herself doing it. The ache in her wrists disappeared. Even more importantly, she had welcomed and received an aspect of God's own image in herself, an expression of God's own artistry. Only so could she freely claim it for her own well-being and offer it for God's purposes in the world. Art soon became a part of her ministry to others.

Karen had been carefully taught to subvert the divine love for her by rejecting the "unimportant" parts of herself. We may begin by accepting a quality within ourselves for our own happiness and well-being—"for our own sake," using a term of Saint Bernard (a twelfth-century monk)—but that very quality is linked, however obscurely, to a quality of the divine Being. Karen's talent quickly became available "for God's sake," through her own ministry. Loving and using a divine part of ourselves probably will lead us out of self-preoccupation to service, for any good quality comes from God and is a road to God.

The need for compassion applies specifically to the parts of ourselves that are genuinely difficult or dangerous. . . . So closely aligned is the love of other parts of ourselves and the love of other people that we can get a clue on how to love the difficult parts of ourselves by practicing on people we find difficult. ("Love" here doesn't mean affectionate feelings but an active intention for the other person's well-being and an openness to see another with compassion.)

One evening, after a discussion on claiming our own experience of God, a participant cornered me with a list of not-so-subtly hostile questions. Why was I giving so much credit to people's experiences? Wasn't it my duty as a priest to tell people the truth rather than trust the ill-informed opinions of the mob? What was wrong with the church these days? Why did they always want to change everything?

At first I felt simply put off. Warm and toasty from a smoothly running session in which most people had participated enthusiastically, the last thing I wanted was this squeaky wheel. But there I was, every inch the priest in full dark suit and collar, and I knew I needed to listen. So I breathed deeply, let go of my annoyance, and tuned in to the woman, listening not only to the words but also to the feelings behind the words. On the surface I sensed the anger—cold, clear, well spoken, and deadly quiet. Behind the anger I began to catch the undercurrent of sadness. A person of deeply conservative convictions, this woman found herself in a church that had changed radically in a liberal direction. Church traditions precious to her had been derided and discarded. I began hearing the plaintive groan behind the cascade of complaints. As I heard that, my compassion was aroused, and I was able to begin telling her I could understand her distress over these losses. I finally glimpsed, behind her anger and sadness, a deep and unspoken hurt. Her church had betrayed something important to her spirituality.

I can't claim I did a very good job of mollifying her, much less helping her to a better frame of mind. But I did befriend her sadness and hurt. She knew she was really being listened to, not dismissed.

That experience led me to respond differently to myself the next time I heard myself bursting out in a torrent of cold, angry complaining. The image of that woman came up in my mind, and I heard her own voice in mine. That realization broke the stride of my abrasive complaint, and I began to wonder what the hurt behind my anger might be. Finding it, I could murmur "you poor thing" to myself by way of comfort, get a more accurate bead on my reasons for distress, and return to deal with people I had flared at with a calmer and clearer head.

We often dislike most vehemently the qualities in others that we are most afraid of in ourselves. Could it be that in the mystery of grace we are to learn something about ourselves from the difficult people who cross our paths? I am, for example, enormously annoyed by rudeness or lack of consideration. "How dare people act that way," I used to fume. And yet, truth be told, I am very haphazard in my consideration of other people. Seldom actively rude, I do not consistently deliver the ordinary niceties that make people feel they are being dealt with courteously. My "thank-you's" are spotty; I ask people to do things and do not sustain them with regular praise and support; and I sometimes get so enthusiastically caught up in what I'm doing that I don't pay sufficient attention to other people's agendas. So I have learned to use other people's rudeness as an occasion for reflection, not just on their behavior but on mine: *Oh, this is what it feels like to be treated that way . . . hmm; maybe they're just haphazard or preoccupied like me. . . . Nonetheless, please note for future reference: it doesn't feel good.*

With such ruminations we befriend a difficulty in a way that leads to genuine repentance and growth as well as enlarges our heart's capacity to bear with the faults sympathetically. This response does not preclude our deciding to challenge someone else's bad behavior. It makes it more likely, however, that our challenge will be clear and clean, not distorted by unconscious projection of our own faults on others.

Only by blessing these inner parts of the self can we come to wholeness of life. By accepting them, we are freed to love others with our whole heart.

THE PERSPECTIVE FROM BELOW
Dietrich Bonhoeffer

Most people learn wisdom only by personal experience. This explains, first, why so few people are capable of taking precautions in advance—they always fancy that they will somehow or other avoid the danger, till it is too late. Secondly, it explains their insensibility to the sufferings of others; sympathy [or compassion] grows in proportion to the fear of approaching disaster. There is a good deal of excuse on ethical grounds for this attitude. No one wants to meet fate head-on; inward calling and strength for action are acquired only in the actual emergency. No one is responsible for all the injustice and suffering in the world, and no one wants to set himself [or herself] up as the judge of the world. Psychologically, our lack of imagination, of sensitivity, and of mental alertness is balanced by a steady composure, an ability to go on working, and a great capacity for suffering. But from a Christian point of view, none of these excuses can obscure the fact that the most important factor, large-heartedness, is lacking. Christ kept himself from suffering till his hour had come, but when it did come he met it as a free man, seized it, and mastered it. Christ, so the scriptures tell us, bore the sufferings of all humanity in his own body as if they were his own—a thought beyond our comprehension—accepting them of his own free will. We are certainly not Christ; we are not called on to redeem the world by our own deeds and sufferings, and we need not try to assume such an impossible burden. We are not lords, but instruments in the hand of the Lord of history; and we can share in other people's sufferings only to a very limited degree. We are not Christ, but if we want to be Christians, we must have some share in Christ's large-heartedness by acting with responsibility and in freedom when the hour of danger comes, and by showing a real sympathy that springs, not from fear, but from the liberating and redeeming love of Christ for all who suffer. Mere waiting and looking on is not Christian behaviour. The Christian is called to sympathy and action, not in the first place by his [or her] own sufferings, but by the sufferings of [others], for whose sake Christ suffered. . . .

There remains an experience of incomparable value. We have for once learnt to see the great events of world history from below, from the perspective of the outcast, the suspects, the maltreated, the powerless, the oppressed, the reviled—in short, from the perspective of those who suffer. The important thing is that neither bitterness nor envy should have gnawed at the heart during this time, that we should have come to look with new eyes at matters great and small, . . . that our perception of generosity, humanity, justice and mercy should have become clearer, freer, less corruptible. We have to learn that personal suffering is a more effective key, a more rewarding principle for exploring the world in thought and action than personal good fortune. This perspective from below must not become the partisan possession of those who are eternally dissatisfied; rather, we must do justice to life in all its dimensions from a higher satisfaction, whose foundation is beyond any talk of "from below" or "from above." This is the way in which we may affirm it.

STREAMS OF MERCY
Mary Rose O'Reilley

It's been my blessing to live among the unfashionable animals—
sheep, rabbits, ducklings, mice—first as an agriculture student and
now as an apprentice in wildlife rehabilitation. In this humble world, I
am learning to forget the great and complicated names of God. When I
was studying spiritual direction at Shalem Institute, Tilden Edwards
gave us a retreat exercise—to sing out the word for God that came
most naturally to us. "Mercy," I sang. As we get older, perhaps, we
shed ideas and concepts until only a few simple words remain.
Mercy remains. The rehabilitation clinic—this abandoned corner of
the universe, with its filth and cockroaches—has become my cloud
of unknowing.

"We save everything we can," I explain to a group of friends
gathered for an afternoon music rehearsal who have asked about my
life as a wild-animal rehabilitator.

They are thinking, I soon realize, of *prestigious* wildlife, the sort our governor occasionally releases to great fanfare on state occasions: the hawk, the eagle, the peregrine falcon—*manly* birds, if I may put it that way. These animals are tended at a beautiful, well-funded facility, the Raptor Center, across the street from where I work. But in our underfunded world of wildlife rehabilitation, a "release" may mean packing up a crate of eastern cottontails, driving them into the country, and watching their panicky break for freedom. No television crews show up for that.

When I tell my friends about the squirrels with neurological damage or the crows needing their feathers reseeded, they are astonished. "You save *everything*?"

Everything. My job last evening was to carefully tuck a mash of fruit and "zoo biscuit" behind the broken teeth of a woodchuck who had been hit by a car. Intubating Canada geese (a four-handed job), chucking pills past the serrated bills of mallards—these are the jobs of an apprentice wildlife rehabilitator.

Back in the human world, I gather with my friends on Sunday afternoons to sing the old gospel repertoire of shape-note music, the texts of Isaac Watts, Charles Wesley, and their company. We are always crying, in four-part a cappella harmony, for God's mercy.

Beneath the sacred throne of God
I saw a river rise;
The streams of peace and pard'ning love
Descended from the skies.[1]

I wail the alto. I think about how I've learned to read the pain of animals, often a *shrinking* that the brain commands, though the body cannot obey. The caged woodchuck, incisors broken, jaws misaligned, is denied the pleasure of bite. He fears me; in a certain sense he hates me—or thus I interpret the white, terrible shriek he lets out when a few calories hit his nervous system and he gathers himself to let me know what he thinks of suburban life, automobiles, and me.

As I feed him, a couple of the veterinary students who direct my work gather around, trying to decide how much suffering is too much, whether the animal is beyond help or too crippled to survive in the wild. Rehabilitate and release is the ethic I've been taught. Sometimes we can place a hopelessly damaged animal—one who is deaf or blind, for example—in a zoo or wildlife sanctuary, but typically space is at a premium for "common" animals. They must be euthanized.

"But we can't save everything, really," I tell my music friends.

※

The faun, about the size of a two-year-old child, but lighter, rests in my arms. Its weight leans into my flesh. It snuggles out of fear rather than comfort. I know it will not be able to live. A young woman sobbing hysterically had thrust the faun, wrapped in a bloody blanket, at me as I came out the front door for a break. As I fold back the blanket I see that the deer's foreleg hangs by a thread.

"Someone hit it with a hay mower," she sobs. "Can you help it?"

If only I could offer her a cup of tea. She is pale and as shocky as the faun. "Why don't you sit down and in a minute I'll bring you some paperwork, but now I'll take the deer back to the doctors."

Jim, a vet student, responds to my soft call. "This animal is badly hurt," I tell him.

"What's wrong?"

"Leg amputation."

"He won't make it then. Why don't you sit back there with him while I find Mark." Mark is our supervising veterinarian.

I hold the placid faun and try to memorize it, as the Navajo teach their children to do. At the clinic, we have been trained like monks in custody of the eyes, in silence never to startle or disturb the animals. "I love the wild no less than the good," Henry David Thoreau wrote of the woodchuck that crossed his path.[2]

Yet it seems fair to make an exception and ponder this beautiful animal. In my other life, studying ceramic sculpture, I am experimenting with a wash of glazes in brown, deep red, black, and sand—the background against which all life but our own hides and rests from the human explosions of color and noise. *Be still and know that I am God.*

Mark materializes and lifts the faun from my arms. As he unwraps the blanket, the deer's leg comes away. I've worked in hospitals and homeless shelters where there always is a lot of fuss and exclamation from staff and client alike, as though the duty of humankind were to comment and keep up a running analysis. But here we learn our discipline from the silence of animals. My daughter said to me recently, "I must be getting deaf. I can't hear you when you talk any more." We speak as little as possible at the clinic, and we take our cues from the green heron, coyote, and terrapin. Cradling the deer, Mark carries it to the gas tanks in the corner and slips a mask over its face. The deer looks puzzled and sleepy as its spirit slips under. Its spirit is, as Thomas Merton wrote of a wild encounter, "the deerness that sums up everything and is saved and marvelous."[3] I go back to the woman in the outer office, busy with forms. "Will it be okay?" she wants to know.

"The vet is with him now" is my evasive reply.

"Can't a deer live with three legs?" one of the new volunteers wants to know.

"Hoofed stock," Jim begins formally, "put so much pressure on the digital phalanges that the bones of the remaining feet would begin to protrude above the hoofs and it would be very painful. Sheep can do well on three feet, but deer cannot."

Come thou fount of ev'ry blessing
Tune my heart to sing thy grace;
Streams of mercy never ceasing. . . [4]

Several years ago, when I was raising sheep, all of us workers, mostly Evangelical Lutherans, used to ponder the imagery of the Good Shepherd. As a former farm kid, you'd think I'd have had enough of Psalm 23, but it remained an icon and a puzzle. In the Buddhist tradition, the Boddhisatva of Compassion is often imaged with a nest of rabbits at her feet. The same year I raised sheep, I studied at a Mahayana Buddhist monastery, Plum Village, where I was given the dharma name "Tending of the Source"—a koan offered me to think about forever, in recognition of and challenge to my shepherd's work. "May all beings be brought to enlightenment," Buddhists pray.

We try to save everything. Even the unfashionable animals. Streams of mercy, never failing.

Merton again, on quail: "Signs of life, of gentleness, of helpfulness, of providence, of love."[5]

Pure intelligence, framed in a silver triangle. Predators have to be smart, wildlife biology teaches me, and I reflect on this fact as I peer into the gray fox's cardboard lair. She has already trained us to put dog food in front of her—no mice, thanks. The fat rodents we fed her yesterday remain in her dish and I remove them from the right like a good servant. This fox came to us after jumping off the sixth floor of a parking ramp downtown while being pursued by an animal control officer. The fall, or flight, did her little apparent harm—in fact, she is pregnant—and she will soon go back to her native habitat. But where might that be? Sixth and Wabasha in downtown St. Paul? The rules of our shelter dictate that animals be returned to where they were found if possible, so they can reconnoiter with family groups. But where is her den? I imagine her traveling by night, past the public library, Mickey's Diner, a shadow making it up the river bottoms from points east.

If predators are pure intelligence, prey gets to be foolish. I tent the rabbit's thin flesh with thumb and second finger and inject her with steroids. She gives me a rabbit's perennial red-eyed multiplex stare. Rabbits have almost 360 degrees of vision, the better to anticipate trouble from all directions—as you have to do if you are at the absolute bottom of the food chain. Next to me a blond clinic worker, braids wrapped around her head, is feeding grubs to a nighthawk that she has wrapped in a soft washcloth (what we call a "nighthawk burrito"). My own next task will be feeding infant bats. It's hard to remember that these intricate little demons are in fact mammals, and we feed them formula through a tiny flexible tube that they suck greedily.

"*Bats?*" my music friends question. Some confess to hitting them with tennis rackets. In the dark neighborhoods around us, robins bounce off the hoods of cars, squirrels turn to leather under our wheels. What's a bat or a rabbit in a nation that's bombed other countries?

"Mercy, O thou Son of David!"
Thus poor blind Bartimeus prayed.
"Others by thy grace are saved.
Now to me afford thine aid."[6]

People speak of the problem of suffering: how could a good God permit the conundrums of violence? By contrast, I am obsessed with the unfathomable problem of mercy: how could a fallen world unspool this golden thread? In dark alleys of our city, people hurt and maim, while in our clinic, people line up to save things. Merton, in his last journals, struggles with the relentless dialogue between action and contemplation, retreating deeper into solitude to find God in a migrating flock of pine siskins. He senses "total kinship with them as if they and I were of the same nature and as if that nature were nothing but love. And what else but love keeps us all together in being?"[7] A tattooed biker comes in with eight mallard chicks he's retrieved from a millrace. He fills out the paperwork with barely literate concentration and buys a T-shirt. A yuppie-looking man brings in a half-dead fledgling, donates fifty dollars, and demands a full report in the mail—his eye too is on the sparrow. Here is a young girl with the face of a born saver. She does not want to relinquish a newborn bunny she has gotten away from a cat. I explain to her about the impossibility of aiding it without extensive equipment, about the dangers of tularemia, and finally, regretfully, I tell her that it's against the law to raise wild things without a license. Along with her paperwork, I give her sign-up forms to volunteer. "You'll have to have a series of rabies shots . . ."

She'll be there at eight a.m.

"We try to save everything."

She nods.

What else but love?

THE COMPASSION OF GOD
Wendy M. Wright

To presume to speak of the nature of God, even of a quality of God's nature such as compassion, is a bold undertaking. To presume to know something of ultimate mystery, one must also be aware of all that one does not know.

Yet there are hints. There are signs and showings. We have our own experience, we have the witness and reflection of faith communities; we have the words of scripture and the lives of the holy men and women. We have the hints, the signs, and the showings.

It is the fall of 1974. I am sitting curled up in an overstuffed armchair in the guest room of a comfortable, vintage-1920s retreat house in the isolated foothills of southern California. The generous windows frame an olive green and burnt sienna landscape flecked with the grays of the thick, dry underbrush; the eucalyptus and scrub oak. The bright gold of the sun is turning to purple in the crevices of the hills. From a portable tape recorder on the bed to my left the voice of a local Franciscan priest is commenting on the first letter of John (3:20).

It has been a tiresome pilgrimage to this remote and quiet moment. Divorce, relocation, returning to school, depression, bouts of meaninglessness, painful self-examination have gutted me empty. I identify with the voiceless, purposeless presence of the trees outside. The priest's voice suddenly comes into the center of consciousness. "God is greater than your own accusing heart," he quotes. Then he elaborates on this phrase, returning to it again. "God is greater than your own accusing heart."

In the gutted center of my consciousness the phrase takes root. I see—no, I experience—the truth that my pain, my confusion, my sense of failure is surrounded and embraced by a compassionate presence *greater* than myself. It is *my* heart, not God's that continues to offer accusation, that mercilessly judges. God steps forth as loving arms, as the patient, longing heart of a mother aching to gather her children in and hold them, to speak wordlessly with the tender pressure of hand and breast of their beauty, dignity, and belovedness.

I begin to know the compassion of God. Greater and more generous than our own knowing, our own evaluations, our own tidy and fearful categorizations, it pursues and overtakes us like a fretful mother or a concerned father. It follows us and finds us wherever we are.

I love the biblical narrative of Jonah because it tells the story of such a God, a God who so loved the people of Nineveh that a would-not-be prophet was hounded down to warn them of the disastrous consequences of their present attitudes. This was a God who ached to have them come back home, so tried to speak to them through Jonah. However, Jonah was reluctant and tried to run away. But God ran after Jonah. God followed Jonah to the bottom of the sea, into the belly of a sea creature, the seemingly most remote of spots, and took Jonah, as it were by the ear, and sent him off on God's errand of mercy. Having heard God's message, the Ninevites responded to God's desire. They turned their hearts homeward and were joyously welcomed back.

I love the story because God's compassion was greater than both the ignorance of the Ninevites and the arrogance of Jonah. Jonah, righteous man that he was, was as skeptical and as judgmental as most of us are prone to be. He resented God's forgiveness of the prodigal Ninevites, resented that they, who were so unworthy, should be spared. Yet God's compassion was greater than Jonah's accusing heart. It stretched wider and deeper than he or we can conceive. Divine compassion follows us into the hidden valley of our arrogance and into the ignorance of our faithless, fragmented lives. It follows and finds us.

∞

It is the middle of the night, June 28, 1985. I am standing awkwardly, leaning over the side of a hospital bed in the labor room at Brigham and Women's Hospital in Boston. My husband is sitting in an armchair across the room looking at me questioningly. I have been in and out of labor for a couple of days now and they have just told us to go back home. It could be a long time before this third baby decides to arrive. But I am in considerable pain. Something feels wrong to me even though I am not at all dilated.

With two previous cesarean sections, one preceded by a long, debilitating labor, I have a hope that we might have this child by a normal delivery. But I have misgivings as well. I am assured by the medical personnel at this high-tech institution that the newest studies indicate no increased chance of uterine rupture after repeated cesareans (especially if the incision is lateral, as is mine). I don't like the thought of major surgery again. The recovery is too hard, and there are risks in any surgical procedure. But everything is so slow. And there is so much curiously situated pain. I try to compare it to the early labor of the other two times. A sense of foreboding, of something not right, fills me. I try to chase it away.

I bide my time. I am afraid to go home. But I certainly do not want to hang around this place racking up costs for another few days. I am aware once more of the terrible, unretractable quality of childbirth. There is no way to postpone, no way to opt out, no way to change your mind now. Right through the middle. That's the only direction to go. It is the most heightened sense of reality I know.

Several hours go by while I wait to see if the contractions become productive. They certainly are draining my energy, pulling me into a pit of pain that continues to trouble me. A cheery young obstetrician pops in to see me and encourages us to go home. "What if there is a rupture?" I inquire. "Rupture? Oh, that happens only once in a hundred cases." He looks at me with a knowing smile, "That won't happen to you."

I am torn about going. Something tells me this is it, whatever it is. Then the contractions really do pick up, although they continue to be only mildly productive. The personnel agree I probably should stay here although it looks like it is going to be a long hard wait. Hours inch by. Then, what is it that tells me? I don't know. I tell my husband I am opting for another cesarean. It is not working. Something is wrong. "But you're doing so well," he says. "Remember how awful the surgery was before. You wanted to avoid that this time." "I know," I say, "but I'm completely exhausted already. And I don't know why but I have this terrible feeling." The doctor is summoned, and it is agreed that another section should be performed.

As I wait to be prepared for surgery a nurse rushes in. I am told that there will be a delay because another woman who seemed to be having a normal delivery was suddenly in distress. The entire night surgical team was tied up, as was the operating room. More hours creep by. By this time I am in great distress and the peculiar sense of foreboding has increased. It is made more surreal by the nearby drama of survival. Stray attendants periodically stick their heads in to check on me and report on the gravity of the struggle going on down the hall: every available surgeon, anesthesiologist, and nurse seems to be involved trying to save the unknown woman's life. Several times it is reported that her condition has stabilized and then she begins hemorrhaging again.

The hours drag by. The unproductive, relentless contractions have sucked up whatever energy I still have left. I'm not sure at this point that I can face major surgery. But there seems to be nowhere else to go. The pain is so omnipresent that it engulfs all other awareness. Finally, the other woman's dark night has turned to dawn, and I am told they are preparing the room. I dread the impending intrusion on my body but dread some other unknown even more. Where will I anchor myself interiorly for this passage? Because I insist on being awake for the delivery (as I was with my other two children), I need somehow to find a firm psychic footing.

On my back, being rolled down a corridor, my physical energy is so deeply eroded I cannot lift my head or raise an arm to help the attendants lift me. Then I call them forth, one by one, the names of the persons whose love has given me life: parents, husband, children, friends, mentors, students. One by one their presences follow the calling of their names. Like a swiftly gathering circle of dancers that surround me, I feel the unique dynamics of each love as it joins the circle: the entire history of each relationship collapsed in one felt presence. They hover over me, the love we have shared burning in all its intensity, holding me, cradling me, carrying me through the narrow passage I am entering.

Time blurs, is both infinite and of no duration. The bright lights of the operating room. The hovering presences. The worried eyes of my husband to my left that try to smile down at me above the surgical mask he has donned. At one point I am sickened by the anesthesia and vomit helplessly onto my face and hair. The surgeon who has been called in to do the surgery, a younger woman with caring, maternal eyes, looks at me over the cloth that shields me from the sight of the instruments slicing through my flesh. "You made the right decision," she says somewhat shakily. "The uterine scar is pulled paper thin. It's barely hanging together. You wouldn't have had much time left."

Then they bring forth my son, a gasping, beautiful new life, and hold him close for me to touch. The best I can do is slightly turn my head so they run his tender naked body against my cheek and I speak his name for the first time. My husband's shaken voice reaches out to me. "Thank you for my son. I know how much this has cost."

Later, in my hospital room, the slender body of my new baby swaddled close in bed with me, I begin to realize what has happened. A vital, life-giving part of myself, in fact *the* life-giving organ, has been used up, given away in giving new life. I begin to mourn. Tears well up, first at the sense of loss, then at the sense of the "rightness" of the loss. The knowledge that we are here to give life to one another and that the giving comes from the very substance of our own being becomes real to me in a new way. The narrow passageway through dying, in this case the proximity of probable physical death and the reality of the exhaustion of the most intimate generative part of myself, heightens the meaning of the newness lying next to me.

I call up my spiritual director and weep into the phone, words about giving away and being used up and being spent and in all that bringing forth newness, my dying becoming new birth. He listens and comments simply, "I feel like I am in the presence of the paschal mystery." Yes. I know.

Something of God's compassion became real to me in this experience. For I now can never move through the cycle of Holy Week and Easter without reflecting on the process of birthing, which is a self-gift so that new life might come into its own. For God so loved the world that God labored and gave of Herself, that through the blood and the waters of her birthing, we would be given new life. The cross is the compassionate self-gift of God, our Mother, whose own body became the crucible through which all humankind and creation itself receives the gasping, vibrant energy of new life.

Closely linked to this loving mystery of death and dying is the loving mystery of the circle of hovering presences that surrounded me in my passage through death to life. Each of those loves, those relationships, participates in the same mystery: the reciprocal giving and receiving, the shared dance of small dyings that become another's rising and another's dyings that become one's own rising. We are at one and the same time one another's mothers and each other's midwifes, welcoming the vital, creative newness that our loving creates.

It is a chilly Monday afternoon in winter 1990. I am sitting, a Bible opened on my lap, in my living room in Omaha with two other women whose names are Sheila and Sarah. They are Jehovah's Witnesses, and they have been coming here to do "Bible study," as they call it, for several weeks. My family has looked askance at this. "Jenny's mother just shuts the door on these people," my elder daughter reports. "What are they going to say in the theology department when you start coming into class and teaching that Armageddon is near?" my husband teases. My two youngest just resent the intrusion and run into the room breaking into our discussion periodically with doleful tales about so-and-so taking someone else's toy.

I must admit that my fascination with these women and their aggressive missionary faith perplexes me as well. In part it is explainable by the fact that I find all religious traditions fascinating and that whenever I have had the chance I have visited and been energized by

Sikh ashrams, Vedanta temples, Tibetan Buddhist meditation sessions, Greek Orthodox Easter vigils, and Pentecostal meetings.

But another part of my fascination with Sheila and Sarah is with the imagery that animates their religiosity. They hand me little pamphlets at the end of our sessions that depict, in graphic fashion, the [end-times] visions of Isaiah. People of different races, dressed in different ethnic costumes, embrace joyfully. Men, women, and children are shown playing together in an earthly garden of great beauty. Fountains flow with pure water. Fruits and flowers spring up from green meadows. Animals roam unhindered and unharming through waving fields of grain. Pictured there is the Witnesses' version of the terrestrial kingdom of God promised by the prophets. The pamphlets invite the reader to consider the apocalyptic signs of the times that point to the proximity of the advent of this kingdom and to become one of the small remnant of true followers of Jehovah who are alerting all humankind to the coming end of all governments as we know them and with that the end of war, famine, disease, and death.

There is nothing insipid or bizarre about these pictures. In fact, they tug at the deepest springs of the human heart, inviting our participation, fueling our most powerful longings. It is these images, which the rest of the Christian world shares but which are, for the most part, only on the margins of religious consciousness, that arrest my attention. That these images so completely capture the loyalty and imagination of the Witnesses challenges me. These women's every waking moment is energized by a passion for the fullness of things. They wait for the end of the world as we know it with joyful self-abandon. This is like what the early Christians must have experienced, traipsing around, tugging at the sleeves of a preoccupied populace: "Look, look! Look at the hope to which we are called! Look at the fullness of things promised by our God!"

It is true that there is a gulf between me and my visitors that is hard to cross. But I love the way in which their hearts are open to radical hope. It seems to me even more astonishing than the vigorous hope for a world renewed that fires Christian advocates of social justice because it points beyond human hope to the hope of God. For the Witnesses it is not we, through our own efforts, who bring about or help God bring about the fullness of things. It is God who does it.

While I would hesitate, on moral grounds, simply to "leave all that up to God," the Witnesses have brought God's compassion into focus for me. The fervor that they bring to my doorway does jog me out of complacency. Look, look! Look at the hope to which we are called! Look at the fullness of things promised by our God! Like a bowstring pulled taut and held ready to propel the arrow to its mark, this passion of theirs for the fullness of things propels my attention to our compassionate God whose beneficence is imaged in the sensual, fragrant language of the scriptures.

Through the words of our holy books we are imaginatively invited into a reality that confounds our realism and our cynicism. The fullness of all things. The fruition of our most earnest dreaming. Our hearts are created to enjoy these, our minds to comprehend such dreams. Joy unbounded. Love so wide and generous it becomes rapture. Abundance so overflowing it splits like a ripe fig and gushes forth like a geyser. Justice so sure, all creatures join hand and paw to dance its sweetness. God's compassion is imaged for us in the lush, greening prophecies of Isaiah and in Jesus' impassioned preaching of the kingdom.

Who or what is this God whose compassion offers and invites us to such a hope that it takes our breath away? We have hints, signs, and showings. May we take them to heart.

THE PRACTICE OF SUBSTITUTED LOVE
Elizabeth Green

In times of difficulty, illness, or loss, we often tell others that we will keep them in our thoughts and prayers—or, in a phrase I hear frequently: "Hold them in the light." These familiar words, and the caring they represent, are certainly valuable and comforting. But what if we can make an even more tangible offer: to carry the weight of others' grief, pain, or fear for a time so they can meet their challenges in a less encumbered way? And what if we can ask others to do the same for us?

The psychologist Robert Kegan gave a glimpse of such a possibility at a conference I attended several years ago. He shared the story of one of his patients, a woman named Rifka, who dashed into the grocery store one afternoon and came upon a young mother and her mentally challenged son. The two women's eyes met for just a moment, and then Rifka went off in search of her items. But later that evening, thinking about this stranger and her child, Rifka began to cry.

She cried for the child, and for the mother, but mostly she cried for all that had been communicated in their brief instant of eye contact. "I cry tonight," she told Kegan, "so tomorrow she will cry less."[1]

Hearing Rifka's story, I was reminded of a scene in a novel by the English mystical writer Charles Williams. An influential but lesser-known member of the Inklings, C. S. Lewis's literary circle, Williams wrote novels, plays, poetry, literary criticism, and theology.[2] In his novel *Descent into Hell*, a young woman named Pauline is overcome by fear, and her friend Peter offers to carry it for her. "When you think you'll be afraid," he says, "let me put myself in your place, and be afraid instead of you. . . . Haven't you heard it said that we ought to bear one another's burdens?"[3]

But of course Pauline, like most of us, has always assumed a figurative interpretation of the phrase. For Williams, however, Paul's [counsel] to the Galatians—"Bear one another's burdens, and in this way you will fulfill the law of Christ" (Gal. 6:2)—is meant to be taken literally. More than a metaphor, what Williams calls "the practice of substituted love" is a spiritual discipline, an active and embodied form of intercessory prayer. "Compacts can be made for the taking over of the suffering of troubles, and worries, and distresses," he explains, "as simply and as effectually as an assent is given to the carrying of a parcel."[4] Indeed, one of the "inklings" that Williams and his Oxford friends shared, it seems, was a growing sense of the transformational possibilities of this practice in their own and others' lives. In a letter to his wife, Williams writes: "But even to carry what we know—what we have chosen to believe—a little steadily in the world; mentioning it if it seems desirable, and proposing it if there seems an opportunity . . . merely to do that might almost make us 'justified in our existence.'"[5]

Explicit in the writings of early church theologians, this choreography of mutual giving and receiving begins in God and weaves through the fabric of creation. For Christians, of course, such burden-bearing culminates in the Incarnation and the Cross. In Jesus, human and divine come together; his life and death reveal the pattern of the glory and link the web of life with the body of Christ.

At the most basic level, "bearing substitution" can be as simple as talking about our troubles. But our culture of ruthless individuality works against even this shy beginning, encouraging us to be self-sufficient, tough it out, go it alone, suffer in silence. It can feel like a radical act to break from the perky party line and admit, even to family members or close friends, when we are unhappy, worried, distressed, or scared. Yet such honesty can truly lighten the burden of these difficult feelings by giving us company in them.

Heading one morning into a meeting I suspected would be uncomfortable, I admitted my trepidation to a coworker. When the familiar button-pushing began, I was amazed at how much it helped just to have someone else aware that I was having a hard time. Nothing was said—I didn't even roll my eyes at my confidante—but she knew, and I knew that she knew. "A little carrying of the burden," Williams writes, "a little allowing our burden to be carried . . . this is the beginning of the practice. The doctrine will grow in us of itself."[6]

Starting to see the connections among us cultivates the soil in which seeds of substitution can be planted. Such unity is not a new idea—Jesus prayed that we might "become completely one" (John 17:23), and Paul proclaimed that "there is one body and one Spirit" (Eph. 4:4)—but we may not be in the habit of acting as if these statements are actually true.

When I told a recently widowed friend that I was thinking about her, I was surprised by her testimony to the palpable comfort of even this minimal level of silent solidarity. "That really helps," she said. "At a time like this, all you can do is put one foot in front of the other and hope that the ground will be there. When you know other people are caring about you, it's like you don't have to worry about the ground being there." The more we begin to believe that this kind of burden bearing can really make a difference, the more we may be willing to give it a try. Our mere attention to what Williams calls "a life of substitution" will provide plenty of opportunities to practice. "It requires only, I will not say faith," he writes, "but the first faint motions of faith."[7]

As time goes on, our experiments with the practice of substituted love can move from the incidental to the intentional. Just as Peter did for Pauline in Williams's novel, we can make specific offers to carry someone else's fear, sadness, or distress for a certain period. Like imaginal prayer or guided visualization, these commitments require a dedicated time and place, protection against distractions, and a willingness, as the poet Mary Oliver puts it, "to enter the long black branches" of the lives of others.[8] Both the giver and taker of the burden have their own roles and challenges. As Williams puts it:

> *The one who gives has to remember that he has parted with his burden, that it is being carried by another, that his part is to believe that and be at peace. . . . The one who takes has to set himself—mind and emotion and sensation—to the burden, to know it, imagine it, receive it—and sometimes not to be taken aback by the swiftness of the divine grace and the lightness of the burden.*[9]

Jesus, after all, told his disciples, "my yoke is easy, and my burden is light" (Matt. 11:30). Relying on this promise and removed from the situation that is causing the other person distress, the burden bearer can afford to feel the feelings without being overwhelmed by them. In a sense, she becomes what Williams calls "the point at which those burdens are taken over by the Divine Thing which is the kingdom."[10] The person giving up the burden, meanwhile, is free to encounter a demanding situation without the added weight of disabling emotions.

The early church desert fathers and mothers, Williams notes, spoke quite plainly about their literal interpretation of bearing one another's burdens. A man must "suffer, and weep, and mourn with [another] . . . as if he himself had put on the actual body of his neighbour, and as if he had acquired his countenance and soul, and he must suffer for him as he would for himself."[11] But getting our rational post-Enlightenment minds around these ideas can be a challenge. Like many of Williams's characters, contemporary Christians may be more comfortable with poetic creeds and metaphorical miracles than with the disturbing thought that, as he often said, "The thing does happen."[12] But like his fellow Inklings Lewis and Tolkien, Williams seeks to save us from the illusions of modernity that insulate us from the encounter with the Real.

Besides, even scientists have recently begun to admit that there is more going on around us than we can observe with our five senses. In a world of dark matter, alternate universes, and virtual reality, is it really too much of a stretch to believe in the possibility of an invisible transfer of burdens? Surely Williams's friend Evelyn Underhill is right: "We are far from realizing all that human spirits can do for one another on spiritual levels if they will pay the price; how truly and really our souls interpenetrate, and how impossible and un-Christian it is to 'keep ourselves to ourselves.'"[13]

Yet it is equally un-Christian to give ourselves unreservedly. A practice of bearing burdens requires vigilance about the price we are paying and attention to "self-care." Certainly common sense suggests that we start small in terms of both intensity and frequency and confine our efforts to reciprocal relationships with family and friends (or pets) rather than professional or pastoral ones.

From brief encounters in the grocery store to deep soul sharing, this holy dance of substituted love invites us into its complex choreography. Perhaps one of the hardest steps to learn is when to lead and when to follow, when to carry and when to yield. If we're used to bearing burdens, giving them up can feel like loss, and it is—the loss of our illusions of separateness and self-reliance.

In September 2001, wading through national grief particularly palpable in the shadow of New York, many of us experienced the breaking down of barriers among strangers. Business calls frequently began with unguarded sharing about lost or spared friends or family, and there was a lot more chatting in check-out lines, post offices, and elevators. I was also in the midst of a personal crisis then, requiring more assertiveness and strength than I felt I could muster alone. So I emailed my extended circle of strong women, sharing my fear and asking them to help me carry it.

With their support, I made it through a pivotal confrontation, so at the end of a very challenging day I went out bowling with my sister and daughter to relax and celebrate. Failing to heed the prominent signs warning me not to cross the line onto the slippery lane surface, I fell down quite spectacularly, practically landing on my head and promptly bursting into tears.

As my sister walked me back to my seat, the man in the next lane caught my eye and asked if I was all right. Feeling foolish, I tried to give a reassuring smile, hoping not to attract more attention than I already had. With everything else going on, the tumble felt like the last straw—but there I was still trying to hold it together, striving for invulnerability. It's a choice we always have. As Peter tells Pauline:

If you want to live in pride and division and anger, you can. But if you will be part of the best of us, and live and laugh and be

ashamed with us, then you must be content to be helped. You
must give your burden up to someone else, and you must carry
someone else's burden. You'll find it quite easy if you let yourself
do it.[14]

I was still pretty shaken a little while later when the man and his
family were ready to leave. He came over, sat down, and put his arm
around me. "I just wanted to make sure you were okay," he said,
"since we're all one family now." I leaned my head on his shoulder and
gave up my burden. And it was quite easy.

The mystery . . . is that God
in her infinite compassion
has linked herself for eternity
with the life of her children.
She has freely chosen to become dependent
on her creatures,
whom she has gifted with freedom.
This choice causes her grief when they leave;
this choice brings her gladness when they return.
But her joy will not be complete
until all who have received life from her
have returned home and gather together around the table
prepared for them.

—HENRI J. M. NOUWEN, GATHERED AROUND THE TABLE

SUGGESTIONS FOR
CULTIVATING A GOOD HEART

1

Learn to listen, to hear what is really being said. Make eye contact with your conversation partner, and try not to interrupt.

2

Consider another person's situation before your own.

3

Volunteer with an organization that puts you in direct contact with people. Find out which groups do what in your community and match your interests and talents with their needs.

4

Chances are you know someone whose situation is more dire than yours. Remember this person when you start feeling sorry for yourself.

5

Become comfortable with silence. Sometimes the most compassionate thing you can do is provide safe space for someone who yearns to be heard.

6

Realize that while some distress is obvious, other needs might not be readily discernible. Pay attention to the people around you.

7

Instead of telling someone what he or she *should* do, ask what they think the appropriate action might be.

8

Pay attention to the small gestures. During the day you have several opportunities to connect with others in a heartfelt way, from thanking your server at the coffee house to offering your seat on the bus to a pregnant woman.

9

Stretch yourself. Reach out to someone in your daily life with whom you don't usually interact, be it a coworker or a neighbor. Offer to drive a peer to work, or check on the elderly man in your neighborhood who lives alone.

10

Be compassionate with yourself so you can be prepared and ready to help others.

NOTES

SEEING WITH OUR SOULS, Marilyn Brown Oden

1. Joan D. Chittister, *The Psalms: Meditations for Every Day of the Year* (New York: Crossroad Publishing Company, 1996), 26. Ps. 103 cited on p. 21.

2. Andrew Sung Park, *The Wounded Heart of God: The Asian Concept of Han and the Christian Doctrine of Sin* (Nashville, TN: Abingdon Press, 1993), 15–20.

3. David Steindl-Rast, *A Listening Heart: The Spirituality of Sacred Sensuousness*, rev. ed. (New York: Crossroad Publishing Company, 1999), 107–108.

A GOOD CRY, Jan Johnson

Jan Johnson, "Weeping with God as a Spiritual Discipline," *Weavings: A Journal of the Christian Spiritual Life* 19, no. 3 (May/June 2004): 44.

COMPASSION FOR ONESELF, Robert Corin Morris

1. See James Russell Lowell, "Once to Ev'ry Man and Nation," in *The Hymnal 1940* (New York: Church Pension Fund, 1943), no. 519.

STREAMS OF MERCY, Mary Rose O'Rcilley

1. *The Sacred Harp*, comp. Hugh McGraw (Bremen, GA: Sacred Harp Publishing Company, 1991), 569.

2. Henry David Thoreau, *Walden and Civil Disobedience* (New York: Penguin, 1983), 257.

3. Thomas Merton, *Dancing in the Waters of Life: The Journals 1963–1965*, ed. Robert E. Daggy (San Francisco: Harper, 1997), 291.

4. *The Sacred Harp*, 312.

5. Merton, *Dancing in the Waters of Life*, 313.

6. *The Sacred Harp*, 56.

7. Merton, *Dancing in the Waters of Life*, 162.

THE PRACTICE OF SUBSTITUTED LOVE, Elizabeth Green

1. Robert Kegan, PhD, keynote address, "Will Our Faith Have Children?" Conference, Chicago, IL, February 14, 2003. Transcript available online at http://www.episcopalchurch.org/48931_4601_ENG_HTM.htm

2. Charles Williams's novels are *Shadows of Ecstasy, War in Heaven, The Place of the Lion, Many Dimensions, The Greater Trumps, Descent into Hell*, and *All Hallows' Eve*. His notable nonfiction includes *The Figure of Beatrice, Outlines of Romantic Theology, The Descent of the Dove*, and *He Came Down from Heaven*.

3. Charles Williams, *Descent into Hell* (Grand Rapids, MI: Eerdmans Publishing Company, 1937), 98.

4. _____., *Essential Writings in Spirituality and Theology*, ed. Charles Hefling (Cambridge, MA: Cowley Publications, 1993), 211.

5. _____., *The Image of the City* (London: Oxford University Press, 1958), 151–52.

6. _____., *Essential Writings in Spirituality*, 215.

7. Ibid., 211.

8. Mary Oliver, "Have You Ever Tried to Enter the Long Black Branches?," in *West Wind: Poems and Prose Poems* (New York: Houghton Mifflin Company, 1997), 61.

9. Williams, *Essential Writings in Spirituality*, 224.

10. Ibid., 223.

11. Ibid., 210.

12. Dorothy Sayers, "Dante and Charles Williams," in *The Whimsical Christian* (New York: Collier Books, 1987), 185.

13. Evelyn Underhill, *Essential Writings* (Maryknoll, NY: Orbis Books, 2003), 39.

14. Williams, *Descent into Hell*, 99.

GATHERED AROUND THE TABLE, Henri J. M. Nouwen

Henri J. M. Nouwen, "The Vulnerable God," *Weavings: A Journal of the Christian Spiritual Life* 8, no. 4 (July/August, 1993): 35.

Contributors

Melissa Tidwell is a writer who has published short stories, prayers, sermons, and small-group resources. She is currently writing a spiritual memoir.

Marilyn Brown Oden, a United Methodist laywoman and retreat leader, is the author of an award-winning novel, *Crested Butte*, and eight nonfiction books.

Jan Johnson is a writer, speaker, and spiritual director. Her books include *Enjoying the Presence of God, When the Soul Listens*, and *Savoring God's Word*.

James C. Fenhagen is the author of *Mutual Ministry*.

Charles A. Parker is the senior pastor of Metropolitan Memorial United Methodist Church in Washington, D.C., the denomination's national church.

Robert Corin Morris is the founding director of Interweave, an interfaith adult education center in Summit, New Jersey. An Episcopal priest, he is the author of *Provocative Grace: The Challenge in Jesus' Words*.

Dietrich Bonhoeffer, 1906–1945, was a theologian, pastor, and writer who served as a central figure in the Protestant church struggle against Nazism.

Mary Rose O'Reilley is a writer and professor emerita of English at University of St. Thomas in St. Paul, Minnesota. Her book of poems *Half Wild: Poems* (Louisiana State University Press, 2006) won the Walt Whitman Award.

Wendy M. Wright is professor of Theology and holds the John F. Kenefick Chair in the Humanities at Creighton University in Omaha, Nebraska. She writes about the history of Christian spirituality, family spirituality, and women's spirituality.

Elizabeth Green is associate director of Interweave, a community learning center in Summit, New Jersey.

Henri J. M. Nouwen, 1932–1996, was an internationally respected author, priest, and professor.

Amy Lyles Wilson is a writer, editor, and workshop leader in Nashville, Tennessee. An affiliate of Amherst Writers and Artists, her byline has appeared in publications including *The Spire* and *Weavings: A Journal of the Christian Spiritual Life.*